# Follow Me Around™
# Russia

**By Wiley Blevins**

SCHOLASTIC

Content Consultant: Kirsten Lodge, PhD, Associate Professor of Humanities and English, Midwestern State University, Wichita Falls, Texas

Library of Congress Cataloging-in-Publication Data
Names: Blevins, Wiley, author.
Title: Russia / by Wiley Blevins.
Description: New York, NY : Children's Press, an imprint of Scholastic Inc., 2018. | Series: Follow me around | Includes bibliographical references and index.
Identifiers: LCCN 2017030781 | ISBN 9780531234587 (library binding : alkaline paper) | ISBN 9780531243701 (paperback : alkaline paper)
Subjects: LCSH: Russia (Federation)—Juvenile literature.
Classification: LCC DK510.23 .B55 2018 | DDC 947—dc23
LC record available at https://lccn.loc.gov/2017030781

Design: Judith Christ Lafond & Anna Tunick Tabachnik
Text: Wiley Blevins
© 2018 Scholastic Inc.

1 2 3 4 5 6 7 8 9 10 R 27 26 25 24 23 22 21 20 19 18

Photos ©: cover girl: EduardSV/Getty Images; cover background: Reidl/Shutterstock; back cover: EduardSV/Getty Images; 1: EduardSV/Getty Images; 3: Irina Fischer/Shutterstock; 4 left: EduardSV/Getty Images; 6 right: psamtik/Shutterstock; 6 left: Artazum/Shutterstock; 7 left: Komarenko Svetlana/Shutterstock; 7 top right: Gado Images/Alamy Images; 7 center right: Gado Images/Alamy Images; 7 bottom right: Heritage Image Partnership Ltd/Alamy Images; 8 left: Vladimir Smirnov/ZUMA Press/Newscom; 8 top right: ALLEKO/iStockphoto; 8 center right: peredniankina/iStockphoto; 8 bottom right: bonchan/Shutterstock; 9 top: UroshPetrovic/iStockphoto; 9 center: ArtCookStudio/iStockphoto; 9 bottom right: salman_ru/iStockphoto; 10: Kekyalyaynen/Shutterstock; 12: Fine Art Images/Heritage Images/Getty Images; 12-13: Vadim Yerofeyev/Dreamstime; 13: Fine Art Images/Heritage Images/Getty Images; 14: Baturina Yuliya/Shutterstock; 15 left: dimbar76/Shutterstock; 15 top right: Popova Valeriya/Shutterstock; 15 bottom right: Vyacheslav Prokofyev/TASS/Getty Images; 16 left: Marco Rubino/Shutterstock; 16 right: ITAR-TASS Photo Agency/Alamy Images; 16 center: Aleks49/Shutterstock; 17 top left: Artem Markin/Shutterstock; 17 bottom left: YURY TARANIK/Shutterstock; 17 top right: Grisha Bruev/Shutterstock; 17 bottom right: Ivan Vdovin/AWL Images; 18 top: Atlaspix/Alamy Images; 18 bottom left: Fine Art Images/Heritage Images/Getty Images; 18 bottom center: Ann Ronan Pictures/Print Collector/Getty Images; 18 bottom right: Keystone/Getty Images; 19 top: OLGA MALTSEVA/AFP/Getty Images; 19 bottom left: AFP/Getty Images; 19 bottom right: ITAR-TASS Photo Agency/The Granger Collection; 20 top: volkova natalia/Shutterstock; 20 bottom: Irina Fischer/Shutterstock; 21 left: Fine Art Images/age fotostock; 21 right: Anil Anilah/Shutterstock; 22 left: Vladimir Smirnov/TASS/Getty Images; 22 right: NATALIA KOLESNIKOVA/AFP/Getty Images; 23 top left: ITAR-TASS Photo Agency/Alamy Images; 23 center left top: Evgenya Novozhenina/Sputnik/AP Images; 23 bottom left: ITAR-TASS Photo Agency/Alamy Images; 23 right: Africa Studio/Shutterstock; 23 center left bottom: Oleg Nikishin/Epsilon/Getty Images; 24 left: Westend61/Getty Images; 24 right: TanyaRu/iStockphoto; 25 right: Sefa Karacan/Anadolu Agency/Getty Images; 25 left: ullstein bild/Getty Images; 26 left: Planet Observer/UIG/age fotostock; 26 top right: Andrey Rudakov/Bloomberg/Getty Images; 26 bottom right: ITAR-TASS/Getty Images; 27 top: ITAR-TASS Photo Agency/Alamy Images; 27 bottom left: Gyorgy Barna/Shutterstock; 27 bottom right: Nerthuz/Shutterstock; 28 A: avdeev007/iStockphoto; 28 B: Zelenskaya/Shutterstock; 28 C: Oleg Moiseyenko/Getty Images; 28 E: Myskina6/Shutterstock; 28 D: ITAR-TASS Photo Agency/Alamy Images; 28 F: Eugen Wais/age fotostock; 28 G: Sergey Krasnoshchokov/Shutterstock; 30 top left: MargaretClavell/iStockphoto; 30 top right: Leontura/iStockphoto; 30 bottom: EduardSV/Getty Images. Maps by Jim McMahon.

# Table of Contents

USA

Russia

# Where in the World Is Russia?

*Privet* (pree-VYET) from Russia! That's how we say "hi." I'm Ksenia, your tour guide. My name means "hospitality." To show hospitality, we treat friends and visitors in a warm and friendly way. We like to show this by offering visitors bread and salt. I hope to show you my best hospitality as you follow me around my fascinating country.

Russia is the largest country in the world. I mean, it's *really* big! It is so huge, it is located in both Europe and Asia. That means we have a lot of different places to see. So, let's get going!

# Fast Facts:

- **Russia covers 6.6 million square miles (17 million square kilometers). It has one of the longest borders of any country.**

- The Ural Mountains separate the European and Asian parts of the country.

- Russia borders 14 countries, including Norway, China, and North Korea.

- **Russia's coasts touch large bodies of water, including the Arctic Ocean, Pacific Ocean, Black Sea, and Caspian Sea.**

- **The Volga River, Europe's longest river, runs through Russia. For three months of the year, most of the river is frozen.**

5

Kitchen

Dachas are often quiet places, far from the noise of the city.

# Home Sweet Home

I am from Moscow, Russia. I'm an only child and live with my parents in an apartment. We share the kitchen and the bathroom with our neighbors. That's common in Russia. We call these apartments *kommunalka*.

Although we live in the city now, my family is originally from the country. We still have a house, or dacha, there that we go to on weekends and vacations. Most dachas, including ours, don't have running water. We have to get our water from a well. We grow lots of fruits and vegetables there. It's very different from how we live in the city, but very relaxing and fun.

Traditional hats have fur lining for extra warmth.

It's cold in Russia much of the year, particularly in winter. You need to bring warm clothes. I recommend buying a traditional Russian hat. It has flaps that you can pull down and keep your ears toasty. That, with a thick fur coat and boots, will be perfect.

If you like to read, you'll be at home in Russia. We have a lot of great books. My parents buy me about five new books each month. My favorite is a collection of poems by Korney Chukovsky.

Many popular children's books are classics our parents and grandparents read.

Holidays and other occasions mean big meals with lots of family and friends.

# Let's Eat!

Each region in Russia has its own special food. In colder parts of the country, stews and soups are common. Borscht is a type of beet soup traditionally cooked with beef. It is served with sour cream, dill, and green onions. You can enjoy it hot or cold. Another popular soup is made from cabbage. It's a bit smelly but so tasty! If you're daring, try our special chicken foot soup. Or taste our yummy dish that looks like jelly with meat floating in it. It's called *kholodets*.

You should also try our warm dumplings when you visit. As part of your meal, order a plate of thin pancakes called *blini* stuffed with jam, honey, cheese, or meat. *Piroshki*, pastries filled with meat and potatoes, are also delicious. They're a favorite of mine. I always ask for them!

Borscht

Kholodets

Piroshki

We eat our fair share of seafood. One of our most famous seafood dishes is caviar. It's salted fish eggs that come from the Black and Caspian Seas. In movies, you often see people at fancy restaurants eating caviar. But here in Russia, it's cheaper and a lot of people eat it!

Want something sweet? Try *zefir*. I love it! It's a marshmallow treat that can be made with walnuts, berries, or bananas. I also like *kissel*. It's a jelly-like dessert made from berries and topped with fresh cream.

In Russia, we typically begin our dinners with cold **appetizers**. These include many pickled things, such as mushrooms, cucumbers, and fish. We end our dinners with a steaming cup of tea. It is the most popular drink in Russia. Many people have a special teapot called a samovar. It keeps water warm so we can enjoy tea anytime we want it.

Caviar

Zefir

Samovar and tea set

# Off to School

Kids in Russia usually go to preschool from ages three to six. After that, we officially start school at age seven. We attend nine grades of elementary school. Then we choose to go to either a trade school or a high school for two years. Trade schools teach us job skills. High schools prepare us for college. But before entering college, we must take the Unified State Examination. This tests our knowledge and skills in school topics. My cousin took it last year. He said it was very hard!

We start school at about 8:00 a.m. and finish at about 1:00 or 2:00 p.m. I walk home with my neighbor and best *droog*, or friend. Because both of my parents work, my grandmother stays with me when I get home. She lets me watch TV and always has a pastry or other treat for me to eat.

друг
(droog)
friend

One of the first things we learn in school is how to read and write Russian. We use a different alphabet than English. It is called the Cyrillic alphabet. It has 33 letters. Some of the letters look like English letters, but they don't all have the same sound as in English. Other letters look like backward English letters or entirely new letters. A few examples are below. Take a look!

| letter | sound |
|--------|-------|
| А а | **ah** as in f**a**ther |
| Б б | **b** as in **b**at |
| В в | **v** as in **v**ery |
| Г г | **g** as in **g**oat |
| Д д | **d** as in **d**ress |
| Е е | **ye** as in **ye**sterday |
| Ё ё | **yo** as in **yo**ur or **yah** as in **yo**nder |
| Ж ж | **zh** as in mea**s**ure |

# Counting to 10

**Knowing how to count to 10 is important when you visit Russia.**

| 1 | один *(ah-DEEN)* |
|---|---|
| 2 | два *(DVAH)* |
| 3 | три *(TREE)* |
| 4 | четыре *(chih-TEE-reh)* |
| 5 | пять *(PYAHT)* |
| 6 | шесть *(SHAYST)* |
| 7 | семь *(SEEAYM)* |
| 8 | восемь *(VOH-seeaym)* |
| 9 | девять *(DYEH-veht)* |
| 10 | десять *(DYEH-seht)* |

# Baba Yaga: A Fairy Tale

**In school, we read a lot of folk and fairy tales.
One of my favorites is the story of Baba Yaga.**

Long ago, there lived a witch named Baba Yaga. She was as skinny as a skeleton and had teeth made of iron. Her nose was so long that it shook the ceiling when she snored. She lived in a hut deep in the forest. The hut stood on magical chicken legs. Surrounding the hut was a fence made of bones to keep away nosy visitors.

One day, a beautiful girl named Vasilisa crept into the forest.

She was sent there by her wicked stepmother and stepsisters to ask Baba Yaga for fire to light a candle. Vasilisa was afraid because Baba Yaga was dangerous. But the girl had a secret. Before her mother died, she had given Vasilisa a magical doll. "Feed and water this doll, and it will wake and help you," she said. Vasilisa fed and watered her doll before entering the forest. The doll kept her safe on her journey.

When Vasilisa reached Baba Yaga's hut, the witch said she'd give Vasilisa fire, but only if Vasilisa completed some difficult tasks. Vasilisa had to clean Baba Yaga's house and yard, wash the laundry, and cook a tasty meal. She even had to separate seeds from dirt.

Vasilisa did all she could, but she could not finish the work on her own. She gave food and water to her magical doll. The doll awoke and completed the work.

Baba Yaga was fooled at first. But she eventually discovered Vasilisa's secret. When she did, she handed Vasilisa fire in a skull-shaped lantern and sent her away. "I don't want your magic in my hut!"

When Vasilisa returned home, the lantern tipped over and burned down her house. Her wicked stepmother and stepsisters did not survive. Finally free from their cruelty, Vasilisa fled. What happened next? Her beauty caught the attention of the ruler of all the land—the **czar**. He asked Vasilisa to marry him. And the two lived happily ever after.

Kremlin

# Touring Russia

## Moscow: Capital City

Welcome to my city, Moscow. It's the capital of Russia. When you visit, you'll want to go first to Red Square. This spot is considered the heart of my country. Around it, you will see famous buildings such as the Kremlin. This former **fortress** was once the home of the ruler of Russia. But it no longer is. Now it has some of our most important museum treasures in it. Our government meets there, too. Next to it is the beautiful and multicolored Saint Basil's Cathedral.

Its onion-shaped domes are known all over the world.

Just steps away is the tomb of Vladimir Lenin. He was the founder and first leader of the Soviet Union, or Union of Soviet Socialist Republics (USSR). That's what my country was known as for much of the 20th century, before we went back to being called Russia. What makes Lenin's tomb different is that his body is in a glass case. Why? So everyone can see him, of course! You can take a look, too, if you want.

St. Basil's Cathedral

Metro station

Gorky Park

Hop on the Moscow Metro, our **subway** system, and speed around the city. The Metro is not just an ordinary subway. Our subway stations are beautifully decorated with paintings, **mosaics**, and statues. You might even spot a fancy chandelier hanging from the ceiling! Many people call the Moscow Metro the most beautiful subway system in the world. And I agree with them.

Make sure you stop at Gorky Park. It has a lot of places to play soccer, gardens to walk through, and ponds to sit beside and relax. During the winter, we skate on the frozen pathways. It's a lot of fun!

Parts of the Hermitage are beautiful works of art themselves.

Dolphinarium

A puppet at the Large Puppet Theatre

## Saint Petersburg: Large and Modern

About 74 percent of Russians live in cities, so there are many cities to visit. One of my favorites outside of Moscow is Saint Petersburg. This place has had different names in the past, such as Leningrad and Petrograd. A must-see site here is the Hermitage. It was once a palace, but it now houses some of the most famous art in Russia. Don't be surprised if you see lots of cats roaming the rooms of this museum.

About 70 cats guard the Hermitage's treasures from pesky rats.

My two favorite things to do in Saint Petersburg are seeing a puppet show and seeing a dolphin show. Head over to *Zazerkalye*, or the Large Puppet Theatre. This is the place to enjoy a traditional Russian fairy tale play with giant puppets. Then zip over to the *Dolphinarium* to see the dolphins perform. But be warned! You'll need a bathing suit or raincoat there because you're sure to get wet.

## Other Fun Places to Visit

Russia's geography is diverse, and the nation has many protected areas. These **nature reserves** include about 50 national parks. Plants and animals in these areas are kept safe from humans.

As you travel through my country, you'll see several big geographic regions. In the northernmost part of Russia is the **Arctic** desert and the tundra. In the tundra, the ground is permafrost, which means it's frozen year-round. There are no trees, only small shrubs and mosses. South of the tundra is a belt of evergreen forest called the taiga. Keep moving south, and the taiga melts into the forest zone. Here you'll find trees such as oak and elm. South of the forest is the steppe. This treeless area is mainly flat plains and **grassland**.

# Our Fascinating History

Our country has a long history. For a big part of our past, a czar, or emperor, ruled Russia. Ivan the Terrible became the first czar in 1547. Ivan earned his nickname by being a controlling and cruel ruler.

Not long after Ivan the Terrible's rule, the Romanov **dynasty** took control. Romanovs such as Peter the Great and Catherine the Great brought new ideas from

Ivan the Terrible

## Timeline: Russia's History

Catherine the Great

Revolution of 1917

Vladimir Lenin

**700s**

**Slavic people**
Settlers build permanent towns and homes in what is now Russia.

**1613–1917**

**Romanov dynasty**
The Romanov dynasty rules for more than 300 years. Russia becomes the largest empire in the world.

**1905 and 1917**

**Revolution**
Unhappy with the Romanov rulers, groups fight to overthrow them.

**1922**

**The USSR forms**
Under Vladimir Lenin, a new **communist** government is set up.

Europe, made changes to our laws, and expanded Russia's territories.

Revolutions ended czarist rule in the early 20th century. In 1922, the

President Vladimir Putin

USSR was established. This government was communist. It controlled the economy. The USSR lasted about 70 years. Since 1991, we've had a freer democracy.

Soviet soldiers

Mikhail Gorbachev and U.S. president Ronald Reagan

**1936–1938**
**The Great Purge**
Enemies of communist leader Joseph Stalin are killed during his rule of the Soviet Union.

**1941–1945**
**World War II**
Germany invades the Soviet Union during World War II. The Soviet Union helps defeat Germany.

**1945–1991**
**The Cold War**
The United States and the USSR experience great tension in a conflict know as the Cold War.

**1985–1991**
**Mikhail Gorbachev**
Political leader Gorbachev reforms the Soviet government and allows more freedoms. The Cold War ends.

**1991**
**The Russian Federation forms**
The USSR and communist control end. The Russian Federation forms.

# It Came From Russia

So many bears roam Russia—brown bears, polar bears, and more—that they are often used as our national symbol. Russia is also home to Siberian tigers, Amur leopards, wolves, minks, ibex, sea otters, and pikas, which are small rodents.

The most popular Russian toy are *matryoshka* dolls. They are a set of wooden dolls. Each doll is hidden inside another doll. These stacked or nesting dolls are beautifully decorated and fun to play with.

Easter is a popular time for kids to decorate eggs. But in Russia, we have taken egg decorating to the next level. We use both real and wooden eggs, and paint flowers and colorful patterns on them. Long ago, a jeweler named Peter Carl Fabergé made decorated eggs for the royal family. They weren't ordinary eggs. These eggs were made of gold and precious stones. They are still the most beautiful and famous Easter eggs in the world!

Alaska is now a U.S. state, but did you know it was once part of Russia? In 1867, the United States bought Alaska from us for only $7.2 million. The land became a state almost 100 years later, in 1959.

21

Christmas trees can be spotted around Russia during the week between New Year's Eve and Christmas.

The Snow Maiden and Grandfather Frost

# Celebrate!

Everyone loves a holiday, and we have some fun ones in Russia. New Year's Day and Christmas are my favorites. They are only a week apart, so it's a whirlwind of fun. Most people in Russia are Orthodox Christians. We celebrate the New Year first. At New Year's, Grandfather Frost visits. He's our version of Santa Claus. With him is the Snow Maiden. She brings lots of gifts!

For Orthodox Christians, Christmas is on January 7. We usually go to church on that day and visit family and friends.

February March

## Other Fun Celebrations

### Maslenitsa (Pancake Week):

This is celebrated seven weeks before Easter. We feast on blini (thin pancakes) and avoid meat. The blini symbolize the sun.

June 12

### Russia Day: This day celebrates the end of the Soviet Union and the beginning of modern-day Russia.

June

### Velikie Luki International Balloon Meet:

This week-long event includes a competition among some of our top balloon pilots.

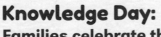

September 1

### Knowledge Day:

Families celebrate the beginning of the school year by bringing their teachers flowers.

## Make Blini

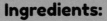

**Ingredients:**

2 eggs, 1 tablespoon sugar, ½ teaspoon salt, ½ cup flour, 2 cups milk, 1 tablespoon vegetable oil, 1 tablespoon butter

**Ask an adult to help!**

**Directions:**

1 Mix the eggs, sugar, and salt in a bowl.

2 Sift in the flour and stir in the milk and oil. Mix until smooth and thin.

3 Heat a lightly oiled frying pan over medium heat.

4 Pour 2 tablespoons of the batter into the pan. Spread the batter evenly around the pan.

5 Cook until the edges look crisp and the center is dry. Then flip with a spatula and cook for another minute.

6 Remove from the pan. Continue making more blini until all the batter is used.

7 Stack the blini, add a little butter in between each one, and enjoy!

Ice-skating

Chess

# Time to Play

Many kids in Russia love sports. Soccer, ice hockey, volleyball, gymnastics, and ice-skating are especially popular. Like many kids in Russia, I take part in youth programs. Not only can we play our favorite sports, we can also learn to dance, sew, and make crafts. Most kids take part in a program after school, on the weekends, and during school vacations.

One of the most popular games is chess. It's a game of skill and **strategy**. We play it in youth clubs, at home, or almost anywhere. When the weather is warm, you can spot a lot of people playing chess in parks and gardens around my country. One of those people would be me! The best chess players are called grand masters. Many Russian chess players have achieved this level. That is my goal, too!

Rudolf Nureyev

Russian ballet company Talarium et Lux performs *Swan Lake.*

My friends and I also like to play a card game called *p'yantisa*. It is similar to the card game called war. The winner is the player who collects all the cards.

In addition to sports, dancing is much loved in Russia. It is an important part of our culture. The Russian ballet is famous all over the world. Russian **composer** Pyotr Ilyich Tchaikovsky wrote some of the most famous ballets in history. *Swan Lake*, *The Nutcracker*, and *The Sleeping Beauty* are among his best-known works. Some Russian ballet dancers, such as Rudolf Nureyev and Mikhail Baryshnikov, have become world superstars.

# You Won't Believe This!

Russia

Alaska

Bering Strait

The Bering Strait separates Russia from the U.S. state of Alaska. At this location, the two countries are only 53 miles (85 km) apart!

Some Russians live in Siberia, which is one of the coldest places on earth. In winter, the average temperature is −10 to −60 degrees Fahrenheit (−23 to −51 degrees Celsius). One day in Oymyakon, the temps dipped to −90°F (−68°C). Brrr!

Russia—called the Soviet Union at the time—was the first country to send someone into space. It happened in April 1961. Yuri Gagarin spent 108 minutes in space as he orbited Earth on the spaceship *Vostok 1*. In June 1963, we sent Valentina Tereshkova, the first woman into space. We also sent a dog named Laika into orbit!

If you like a quick hamburger, Russia is home to the largest McDonald's in the world. The restaurant is in Moscow, and it can seat 700 people!

We only give an even number of flowers (two, four, six, or even a dozen) for funerals. It is considered bad luck to give someone an even number of flowers outside of funerals.

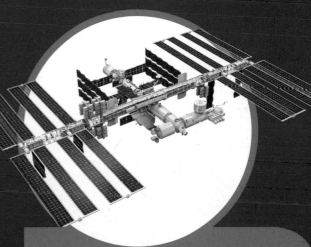

All astronauts on the International Space Station must know both English and Russian. Crew members often speak to one another in a mix of the two languages they call Runglish.

# Guessing Game!

Here are some other great sites around Russia. If you have time, try to see them all!

**A**

This is the oldest and deepest freshwater lake in the world. It has plants and animals that can't be found anywhere else.

**E**

Learn about the Russian space industry at this museum.

① Samara Space Museum
② Valley of Geysers
③ Trans-Siberian Railway
④ Vladimir Lenin head statue
⑤ Sochi National Park
⑥ Mount Mutnovsky
⑦ Lake Baikal

**B**

Take a fun picture in Ulan-Ude with the largest statue head of one of the Soviet Union's great leaders.

**F**

This park near the Black Sea has lots to explore—mountains, canyons, rivers, and caves.

**D**

Visit this large active volcano that erupted as recently as 2000.

This is the second-largest geyser field in the world and a popular stop for tourists.

**G**

**C**

Hop aboard a train for this 6-day, 5,800-mile (9,200 km) trip between Moscow and Vladivostok.

28

# Preparing for Your Visit

By now, you should be ready to hop on a plane to Russia. Here are some tips to prepare for your trip.

❶ Before you come to Russia, exchange your money. Our money is called rubles. Each ruble is made up of 100 kopeks. You'll need plenty of rubles to buy fun souvenirs.

❷ If you're out and about and need the restroom, I recommend you use one of our pay toilets. They are cleaner and more pleasant than the free ones you might find. So bring some extra rubles. Free toilets also don't always provide toilet paper. It's a good idea to have a roll of toilet paper or package of tissues with you in case you end up using a free toilet.

❸ Continue your traditional Russian experience by hopping on a troika during winter. It's a horse-drawn sleigh that's perfect for riding through the snow. You can find one at Shuvalovka, a reproduction of a Russian village from long ago. It's near Moscow. You can also go pony-trekking or dogsledding through more remote parts of the country.

❹ Bring an adapter for your electronics. This plug helps your electronics plug into outlets that are a different shape. Otherwise, you won't be able to plug in your phone or tablet charger. Not good!

❺ It's very cold in Russia in the winter. You'll want to bring a warm coat, boots, a hat, and gloves. But always take your gloves off when you shake hands with someone. If you leave your gloves on, we think it's very rude!

# The United States Compared to Russia

| | | |
|---|---|---|
| **Official Name** | United States of America (USA) | Russian Federation |
| **Official Language** | No official language, though English is most commonly used | Russian |
| Population | 325 million | 130 million |
| **Common Words** | yes; no; please; thank you | da (DAH); nyet (nee-YET); pozh-aluysta (pah-ZHAL-stah); spa-siba (spa-SEE-bah) |
| **Flag** | | |
| **Money** | dollar | ruble |
| **Location** | North America | Asia and Europe |
| **Highest Point** | Denali (Mount McKinley) | Mount Elbrus |
| Lowest Point | Death Valley | Caspian Sea |
| **National Anthem** | "The Star-Spangled Banner" | "Gosudarstvenny Gimn Rossiiskoi Federatsii" |

Now you know some important and fascinating things about my country, Russia. I hope to see you someday exploring one of our national parks, ice-skating on one of our outdoor rinks, or sipping one of our traditional soups. Until then . . . *dasvidanya* (da-svee-DAH-neeyah). Good-bye!

# Glossary

**appetizers**
*(AP-uh-tie-zurz)*
portions of food eaten
before a meal or at the
start of a meal

**Arctic**
*(AHRK-tik)* the area
around the North Pole

**communist**
*(KAHM-yuh-nist)* a
system of organizing the
economy of a country so all
land, property, businesses,
and resources belong to the
government or community,
and profits are shared by all

**composer**
*(kuhm-POH-zur)*
someone who writes
something, especially music

**czar** *(ZAHR)* the emperor
of Russia before the
revolution of 1917

**dynasty** *(DIE-nuh-stee)*
a series of rulers from the
same family

**fortress** *(FOR-tris)*
a place such as a castle
that is built to protect the
people inside it from attack

**grassland** *(GRAS-land)*
a large, open area of grass

**mosaics**
*(moh-ZAY-iks)* patterns
or pictures made up of
small pieces of colored
stone, tile, or glass

**nature reserves**
*(NAY-chur rih-ZURVZ)*
places where animals can
live and breed safely

**strategy**
*(STRAT-ih-jee)* a clever
plan for winning a military
battle or achieving a goal

**subway** *(SUHB-way)*
an electric train or a
system of trains that run
underground in a city

## Index

## Facts for Now

Visit this Scholastic website for more information on Russia and to download the Teaching Guide for this series:

**www.factsfornow.scholastic.com**   Enter the keyword **Russia**

## About the Author

Wiley Blevins is an author living and working in New York City. His greatest love is traveling, and he has been all over the  world. He has written several books for children, including the Ick and Crud series and the Scary Tales Retold series.